Negotiation

Ivan Remus, PE, Esq.

ALL RIGHTS RESERVED

NEGOTIATION - Copyright © 2018 by Ivan Remus, PE, Esq. All Rights Reserved.

All rights reserved. No part of this book may be reproduced in any form or by electronic or mechanical means, including information storage and retrieval systems, without written permission from the author. The only exception is for a reviewer, who can quote short excerpts in a review.

Cover designed by Pro_ebookcovers on Fiverr.com

The examples presented in this book should be considered a work of fiction. The names, characters, places, and incidents, if any, are the product of the author's imagination or are used in a fictitious manner. Any resemblance to real people, alive or dead, events or places is purely coincidental.

Ivan Remus, PE, Esq.
Visit my website at www.IvanRemus.com
You can also visit my professional webpage at www.Ivan-Remus.com

Printed in the United States of America

First Printing: Aug 2018

ISBN-13: 9781730763700

INTRODUCTION

Virtually all aspects of life are affected by the need to negotiate. The car you drive, the house where you live, the clothes you wear, the jobs you have, the salary you earn, the debts you pay, and even the side of the bed where you sleep is the direct product of your ability to negotiate.

So, the obligatory question is, if practically everything in our lives has been directly affected by our ability to negotiate effectively, why is not it taught as a compulsory subject since we are in elementary school?

The general goal of the negotiation process is to meet the needs of the participants called to negotiate. Negotiation should be considered successful only when both parties know and feel that their demands were met.

The above approaches lead us to a second question, if virtually everything in life is negotiated, how can it be explained that some negotiators obtain much better results than others?

The truth is that there is no magic formula. What we can do is identify a series of essential strategies that the most experienced negotiators master and that help them to reach agreements that satisfy all interested parties.

NEGOTIATION

This book explains in detail the steps we must follow to make a successful negotiation, in addition to presenting the twenty-four strategies that exist in the negotiation, which are essential to know how to identify them, as well we can counteract them in those cases in which the other party try to implement them with us.

The negotiation is compared very frequently, with a game. Like games, where there is a set of rules that govern them, the negotiation process has a set of rules and values.

The detail is that if the negotiation is viewed as a competitive game, there is a risk of entering the negotiation process with a seasoned spirit in which only a part hopes to reach the goals set.

Even if we can persuade the opponent to "play our game," we run the risk of being losers instead of winners. The objective must be to reach agreements and not total victories. Each party must know and feel that they have won something. Therefore, negotiation is not a game, let alone war. Our goal is not to have a dead competitor.

Through years of experience as a lawyer, negotiating multi-million dollar contracts, or litigating the most critical points in a legal process, I have learned that a "good lawyer" is not the one who litigates and fights every little detail, but the one who manages to minimize the differences and controversies to the minimal expression. As my wise father used to say: "it is better an agreement which we can live with than a judgment sentence, because, in the first, we were the ones who arrived at those decisions, in the second is a judge who ends up deciding (and imposing) the possible solution to the difference.

The trick is that we should think of negotiation as a cooperative enterprise and not as a game of competition. Remember, we must be wise enough to know how to maintain the objective of our negotiating agenda and not allow our personal agenda of repaying the ego to stand in the way.

If both parties enter into cooperative negotiations, there is a substantial likelihood that they will be persuaded to obtain goals that can be shared equally. This in no way means that each goal will be valued equally by each participant, but that there is a higher possibility of both parties reaching a successful cooperative goal.

The three most important advantages of the cooperative approach are:

1. It allows us to achieve better results.

2. Generates solutions that are more likely to be durable

3. The efforts of both parties are cumulative

Despite the preceding, the negotiator must not wholly abandon the competitive attitude as this allows us to remain alert. As we have already mentioned, many see the negotiation process as a competitive process to take advantage of the other, so even if we want to direct the process towards a cooperative arena, it would be naive for us to think that every negotiator feels in the same way.

Keeping alert and not lowering the guard during the process serves as an integrating process that coordinates the actions of both parties. We must reach that delicate balance in which we allow a healthy cooperative rivalry to exist that coordinates personal actions and those of the opponent.

Have you ever wondered why there are very successful people in business while there are others who, no matter how hard they try, seem

NEGOTIATION

unable to advance their projects? Well then, pay particular attention to all the valuable information contained in this book. If you decide to learn and apply the secrets set forth here, you will begin to succeed and make progress in the areas of your life where you have not seen them before.

CONTENTS

INTRODUCTION	iii
DEFINITION	1
STEPS TO AN EFFECTIVE NEGOTIATION	3
Step 1: Preparation	3
Step 2: Control your Reactions	8
Step 3: Disarm the Counterpart Before Negotiating	12
Step 4: Demonstration of Interests and Needs	16
Step 5: Build the golden bridge	18
EFFECTIVE NEGOTIATING STRATEGIES - NEGOTIATING TACTICS AND DEFENSES	23
Strategy 1: Flinching (The moan)	23
Strategy 2: The Budget	24
Strategy 3: The selection of cherries	25
Strategy 4: The pressure of the date (The offer expires)	26
Strategy 5: Ascent and descent	27
Strategy 6: Upss ...! We already did it or "It's better to ask for forgiveness than to ask for permission."	28
Strategy 7: Deadlock	29
Strategy 8: Good Cop, Bad Cop	30
Strategy 9: The Pressure of Expectation ("You have to do better")	32
Strategy 10: This is my final offer	33
Strategy 11: Higher Authority	34
Strategy 12: Low ball	35

Strategy 13: Freebies (The Salami). — 36
Strategy 14: The Auction — 37
Strategy 15: Take it or leave it — 38
Strategy 16: What if ...? — 39
Strategy 17: The phony problem solver — 40
Strategy 18: The Lure — 41
Strategy 19: Friendship or family relationships — 42
Strategy 20: Discouragement and Indifference — 43
Strategy 21: The commitment — 44
Strategy 22: The Stonewall — 45
Strategy 23: Attacks — 47
Strategy 24: Tricks — 48

THE GOOD HUMOR AS THE UNIVERSAL DEFENSE — 50

B.A.T.N.A.: How to use power as an integral part of negotiation — 52

PSYCHOLOGICAL FACTORS AND HOW TO FACE THEM — 56

WHO HAS THE GREATEST EGO? THE POWER PARADOX — 59

EPILOGUE — 61

BIBLIOGRAPHY — 62

OTHER BOOKS BY IVAN REMUS, PE, ESQ. — 63

ABOUT THE AUTHOR — 64

THANK YOU! — 65

RESOURCES — 66

DEFINITION

When defining what Negotiation is, we must look carefully at the use of the word as a noun and as a verb.

The Oxford Dictionary defines the word **Negotiation** as a noun that comes from Latin (negotiatio, -ōnis) and means:

1. The discussion aimed at reaching an agreement.

2. <u>The action or process</u> of transferring legal ownership of a document. (Emphasis supplied)

Source: https://en.oxforddictionaries.com/definition/negotiation

The Oxford Dictionary also defines the word **"Negotiate"** as a verb, and accepts the following meanings:

<u>Try to reach an agreement</u> or compromise <u>by discussion.</u> (Emphasis supplied)

Source: https://en.oxforddictionaries.com/definition/negotiate

Based on both definitions that the Oxford Dictionary provides us, let us generate our own interpretation of these definitions.

Negotiation is the act of communicating to try to reach an agreement, where some interests are shared and where other interests are opposed.

NEGOTIATION

Negotiating is looking to get from the other person something we need or want convenient. It is the most significant process for making both personal and professional decisions.

The satisfaction of mutual needs is the common denominator in all negotiations. The problem arises when the other party assumes a rigid position, where the other party is only interested in satisfying their needs.

We have highlighted some key words in these definitions. The two keywords are act and process.

It must be entirely clear to us that Negotiation is a process that involves the planning and execution of a series of steps to achieve the success of this process. Let's see what those steps are.

STEPS TO AN EFFECTIVE NEGOTIATION

Step 1: Preparation

The secret to effective negotiation is the preparation. The more difficult the negotiation is, the more preparation is needed. We don't think we are exaggerating when we say that you have to prepare at least one or two minutes for each minute you will interact with the other party.

Dr. Stephen R. Covey in his book "The Seven Habits of Highly Effective People" clarifies in his second habit (Begin with the End in Mind), that it means starting each day, task or project with a clear vision of the desired address and destination. We could not agree more with Dr. Covey. We must have a clear idea of the desired achievements.

Scheduling a preparation session with a friend or colleague is instrumental. It is better when you dialogue the strategy with another person you trust.

In the absence of that third person to help us, we can apply in a very useful way the so-called "Disney Technique", which we explain in detail in our negotiation workshop, as well as in our VIP private consulting group, where we teach to get the most out of this powerful and secret tool for success.

NEGOTIATION

When preparing to enter into a negotiation process, we must take into account the aspects that serve as a **guide for the preparation:**

1. Determine what our interests are, where we want to go with the situation - We must establish a precise position of the objectives we want to achieve. Establishing a position means organizing and clearly defining the specific things we say we want. The interests are the motivations that lead us to take positions. Interest is reached when we ask ourselves, why? The best way is to establish priorities of interests.

For this, we must have clear what is the order of priorities of the goals that we value. Our scale of values clearly defines our criteria when it comes to making decisions. Having clear objectives to achieve helps us establish the way forward in the negotiation process.

2. Determine what the interests of the other party are - We must "put ourselves in the shoes of the other party," we must understand their perceptions. If possible, talk to people who know them; for example, its suppliers, customers, former partners, and so forth. Just as the first criterion is to define what is our scale of values and principles when making decisions, it is impressively powerful to determine what is the scale of values and rules when making decisions of the opposite party in a negotiation process.

In our private VIP consulting group, we provide you

with the specific steps to follow to determine what the interests of the other party are.

3. Look for creative ideas to meet the interests of both parties - invent options for the game. It can be done through brainstorming sessions. It is important to note that by definition, the brainstorming process is a creative process that must be done without criticism. We must identify first and evaluate later.

4. Look for fair and independent standards to resolve differences - standards can be the value in the market of the goods or goods to be negotiated, costs versus benefits, equal treatment, the law, legal precedents, among others.

5. Identify the best group of alternatives or possible solutions if the negotiation fails (BATNA) and identify those of the other party as well as decide whether to negotiate. The real purpose of a negotiation is to explore if you can better satisfy your interests with an agreement instead of making a BATNA (Best Alternative To a Negotiated Agreement), look for an alternative walk away.

The term BATNA was coined by Roger Fisher and William Ury in his book, *"Getting to Yes: Negotiating Without Giving In."*

For his part, Robert Dilts tells us in his book *"The Fourth Position"* that several alternatives must be considered:

a. What can we do on our own to achieve our interests?

b. What can we do directly with the other person to respect our interests? (Ex .: go strike).

c. How can we introduce a third party to the situation (e.g., go to court or arbitration)?

6. Formulate a proposal - This proposal should not be a rigid position but a concrete illustration of the type of result that will best fill our interests and those of the other party. Of course, we should not make the mistake of telling the other party that our position is not a rigid one because we would automatically open the door for someone else to reject our proposal because we believe in their subconscious the impression that they can achieve something more or better of us.

When formulating our proposal, we must clearly define:

a. To what agreement we **aspire,** what will make me happy;

b. What will give me satisfaction?

c. With what kind of agreement **can** we live, even if we do not (like) (And above all, what is the worst that could happen).

7. Practice the strategy with a colleague or friend - Practice is one of the seven laws of the human mind. We usually say that "Perfect practice achieves perfection," however, I prefer to say that "perfect practice significantly improves performance." In our negotiation workshop and our exclusive private VIP consulting group, we have specially designed exercises to practice and develop this important skill.

8. While negotiating, you must also prepare. The preparation does not end when you start negotiating. In summary, in this step, we must apply what is known in Neuro-Linguistic Programming (NLP) as: "The good formation of the desired achievements."

Once we are in front of the person, we must established rapport, which means a good relationship. Moreover, I have news; you only have less than seven seconds to develop a rapport with the person.

Rapport is achieved through the techniques we teach in our VIP negotiation group of "mirroring, and guiding."

Step 2: Control your Reactions

The ancient Chinese philosopher Lao Tzu used to say: "Respond intelligently even to unintelligent treatment."

Isaac Newton would be proud of my phrase: "Actions provoke reactions. The reactions provoke, counter-reactions. "And we really must concentrate on responding and not on reacting blindly.

When dealing with someone difficult:

1. **Do not try to control the behavior of the other party, control your behavior** *assertively responding to the situation instead of reacting.*

2. **If necessary, go to the balcony** Sometimes, that respite can make a big difference. Remember that the door is always open for a break. Ask to go to the bathroom, drink water or smoke a cigarette, even if, like me, you do not smoke! "At that moment alone, relax, breathe. Assume a mental attitude of disinterest as if it were a third part (goal), think constructively on both sides.

How to control reactions:

1. Recognize the tactic: By being able to identify the strategy that is being used against us, we can neutralize the effect of them. The worst thing that can happen to us during the negotiation process is not knowing what they are doing to us while they use it against us.

The most difficult tactics to detect are the lies. The secret to detect them is to look for inconsistencies between the words we hear, on the one hand, and the words previously were spoken. We must also look for discrepancies between words and facial expressions, the tone of their voice and body language. Usually, the liar can not control his facial expressions, nor the tone of his voice.

A subtle characteristic that frequently occurs is the "rascality" or roughness of the throat, which obliges to get rid of it by coughing, due to the tensions that are generated in the vocal cords of the person who is about to say a falsehood. These and other important body language cues are detailed in the VIP discussion group.

2. Take mental notes when detecting a possible attack. It is not putting on the armor; it is putting on a radar. Keep it in mind as a possibility and not as a sure thing. Look for additional evidence based on the belief that difficult people are not limited to a single tactic. To neutralize the effect of the tactics of the other party, we must recognize what we are feeling. We must be particularly aware of small signs like:

   a. Changes in breathing,

   b. Discomfort in the stomach

   c. Does the heart flutter?

   d. The face blushes as a sign that something is wrong and

   e. You lose your composure in the negotiation. Our body speaks to us continuously. Pay attention to him, listen to him. I do not wait for him to scream.

3. Identify and recognize the so-called "Hot Buttons" or possible trigger buttons: If we understand and accept that they exist, we can recognize when the other party is using them. By recognizing them, we control natural reactions. We must be prepared to receive verbal attacks and not take them as personal. Remember that the other person's idea is to make us lose control. Sometimes the idea of seeing the opponent as someone who does not know how to debate ideas helps, so he resorts to his only available tool in the face of his ineptitude, resorting to personal attacks.

4. Gain time to think - We need time to think about how to respond and carry out our strategies. It should be paused in the middle of the attack and avoid responding. In this way, things are seen objectively. If we do not answer, they have nothing to use against us. Remember that our main agenda is to achieve our objectives set at the beginning of the negotiation, and this has nothing to do with our pride. Keep clear the goals of your main agenda.

To avoid reacting in an uncontrolled manner to possible attacks, it is recommended that you:

   a. Do not eliminate feelings, but <u>disconnect the automatic link between emotions and action</u>. Do not channel the impulses in reaction.

   b. <u>Slow down the negotiation</u> – put reverse to the negotiation process by reviewing the discussions, examine arguments . Give yourself time, back the mental videotape to recognize the tricks and neutralize its impact. One way to slow down is to take notes of what the other party is talking about, in this way you show them that you are taking them seriously while making time.

Sometimes looking a bit slow is preferable. Requesting a break or Time Out for both parties helps a more productive negotiation.

Time Out can be obtained by looking for an excuse, such as "Let's go for a coffee break." A reasonable justification is to call a caucus in your group, with the explanation that they obtained new information. They have no idea how many times I have asked the judge for time to consult with my client or to go to the bathroom while I am in the middle of a negotiation process.

Another way to gain time is to integrate another negotiator, while one speaks the other has time to think. It gives you the double benefit of adding a different perspective to our approach while providing a break in each relay of who carries the leading role of negotiation.

NEVER make an important decision on the spot. If you have to do it at the moment, take the time with the excuse of making a phone call, or going to the bathroom, for example. You can not fall in a hurry. Your worst enemy is being hurried. Moreover, remember:

Don't get mad,

Don't get even,

Get what you want....

Step 3: Disarm the Counterpart Before Negotiating

It is a grave mistake to try to reason with a person who is not receptive. Before discussing the problem, you must disarm the person. Disarming them means diverting their hostile emotions, making them see our point of view and gain respect from the other party.

The secret to disarm is to surprise. Do the opposite of what another person expects from you. The opposite of putting pressure on the other party is to take him to a constructive interaction, listen to him, agree as many times as possible, see the situation through his eyes.

To break the resistance, you have to reverse the dynamics. If we want to be heard, we must start by listening to our contra part, recognizing them and agreeing with them.

Strategies to disarm:

1. Listen - perhaps the least they expect is to be heard. We satisfy the need to be understood by not interrupting them, maintaining eye contact, and creating empathy. It is not just listening to them, but letting them know that we understood the message, by repeating the words, summarized, but keeping the point of view of the person (paraphrasing). Listening to them gives us the opportunity to know that we understood correctly. Moreover, we get the person to say the magic word. (Later you'll know what we mean).

2. Recognize them - does not mean we agree with the other party, but let them know that we accept their point of view. This can be done by saying, for example, "this is the way I see it, of being in your shoes." Also, we must recognize their feelings, for example: "I feel that you feel annoyed because you think we are taking advantage, I understand."

The most powerful way to recognize is to offer an apology as it creates the conditions for a constructive resolution of a dispute, you can say: what can we do to correct it?"

3. Be genuinely in agreement - Project trust, even non-verbally. Do not counter-attack. When listening, for example, you have a point. Change the mode of the conversation.

The last place they would expect us to see is to be on their side. **It is very difficult to attack someone who agrees with us.** We must focus on the points in common. We must wisely use a good sense of humor.

4. The Keyword is "Yes." Look for occasions in which the other party can say "yes"> you achieve this with suggestive questions, that accept only YES or NO answers, and that the other party can only respond with a "YES."

5. Calibrate, pause and establish Rapport continuously: See how the other party communicates and look for tuning in the same line, pairing its intensity and mode. For example: if you speak in a low tone, you also lower your voice. The goal is to tune in with the other person.

You must be sensitive to the way you express yourself. This is particularly important when dealing with a person from another culture or country since words could have very different meanings. What for someone could be completely innocent, could turn out to be very offensive and insulting to the other person.

If the person uses mainly **visual** phrases, try to match the sentences: *"Yes, I SEE your point of view." "I can SEE what you say."* On the other hand, if the person uses mainly **auditory** phrases, like saying, *yes I'm listening ...* The purpose is to connect by using the language that the counterpart better understands.

6. The personal validation disarms: Satisfy the ego of the one who needs recognition. You can build a personal relationship that works - invite him to a café and talk about hobbies to show personal respect and goodwill. The best way to establish a good relationship is before a problem arises.

7. Use the structure "<u>Yes, and</u>" versus the common structure of "<u>Yes, but</u>": It's very common for us to express the difference with a BUT. The problem with the word "BUT" is that it anticipates a contradiction. We can recognize the point of view of the other party and without challenging it, express a different point of view. For example: *"Yes, you are correct, and it adds better service ... "* You do not have to make them look bad, for us to look good.

Pay attention to the following example and contrast how you feel about the following two sentences:

   a. That yellow shirt looks very nice on you, **and** the blue one looks even better.

   b. That yellow shirt looks very nice on you, **but** the blue one looks even better.

In the first sentence, we are telling you that both shirts look pretty. In the second sentence, we are telling him that in reality, only the blue shirt fits you well. This is why is so important to use a sentence structure where we use the "AND" instead of the "BUT."

8. Instead of attacking, express feelings and experiences. This is what is known in English as the "I statement" which sends the same message but expressing feelings in this way, tend to be heard more. It is about describing the impact of the problem on you, giving the other party information about the consequences of their actions in a way that is difficult for them to refuse. This position does not challenge; it only offers a different perspective.

You can support the other and maintain our point of view. It is important to realize that showing support to the other does not mean losing our position. It is to assume favorable positions at the same time that we believe that a positive solution is POSSIBLE.

9. DO NOT reject, Restate: Instead of dismissing what the other party establishes, we must accept it and transform it into the negotiation we want to have. Re-framing (Reframe) is directing what the other party says in a way that leads attention back to the search to satisfy the interests of both parties; it is about redirecting the attention of the conversation towards the final objective. Remember, your main agenda is to achieve the negotiated objectives of the negotiation, and it is not to compensate your ego.

10. CHANGE THE FRAME AROUND THE IMAGE: In other words, put a framework to solve problems around the positions of the other party. To change the focus of attention, to be focused on the things that we disagree, to a focus on the positions that benefit both parties. Remember, it is very difficult to argue with someone who shares our position.

Our job is to change the focus of positions to open interests that seek to solve problems (ask them what they think). Treat the other party's position as an opportunity, rather than an obstacle and focus it through questions. These questions reveal.

Step 4: Demonstration of Interests and Needs

An insistent demonstration of interests and needs helps to produce an agreement that satisfies both parties.

How we formulate our questions is as important as **what** is being asked. My grandmother always said: "It's not what you ask, but how you ask and to whom you ask." Moreover, every day I am more convinced that my wise grandmother was right, the questions must show interest and respect towards the other party. For this we must:

1. **Identify the other party's interests** - If the other party does not want to disclose their interests, the focus should be changed. Usually, people of this type tend to criticize excessively. You can ask them to correct you. *"If I do correctly understand, your interests are ..."* Few people tolerate not correcting others.

2. **Involve them to discuss possible options** – Use the "what if?" What if….? It can be taken as a brainstorming session ... In a marriage that does not agree where to spend the Christmas holidays: "What if we spent Christmas at my parents' house and New Year with yours ...?" Invent first and evaluate after…

3. **Ask for the advice of the other party** – Ask: "What do you suggest?" They will never wait for these kinds of questions. It disarms them, and at the same time, it gives us the opportunity to educate them about the problem.

4. If the other party's position does not change, instead of rejecting them, **ask, what makes it fair?** Say something like: "You must have your reasons to think that your solution is just, I would love to hear them." That way we go beyond the questions, and we also establish

fair standards. A question to solve a problem must be an open question (that it can not be answered merely with a "yes" or a "no." The answer we receive will depend on how the question is asked. To ask a question that can not be answered with a yes or no, we must begin our question with:

    a. How?

    b. Why?

    c. Who?

Ask questions for which the other party may not have an answer. In those cases, you should be helped to break the silence, asking them follow-up questions, that way we will eventually respond.

Step 5: Build the golden bridge

Very often there are "impasses" in the negotiation process. Resistance can come in several forms:

a. Lack of interest in your proposals.

b. Vague positions.

c. Arrears.

d. Renege agreements.

e. A big fat NO!

Among the most common reasons for an *"impasse"* we have:

a. **It is not their idea**.

b. **The proposal does not comply with the fundamental interests** of the counterpart

c. **Fear of losing or looking bad** – Nobody wants to look bad in front of the opponent. Possibly, the other party does not want others to know that he surrendered at some vital point of his requests. As a negotiator, you have to help him look good for his people. Remember, everyone wants to maintain their self-worth, their dignity, their sense of honor, their desire to act consistently with his or her principles and the desire to look good in front of others.

d. **The pace is too fast** – If you ask for a lot, very quickly, it is easier to say NO. Our job is to make the process more comfortable for the other party, for this, we must:

i. Break the decision into small pieces or steps – Remember the saying: "Bite a bite we eat an elephant." Each partial agreement can lead to a total consensus, start with the most straightforward points and on which we are sure there will be agreements.

ii. Do your part of the work.

iii. Seek to generate momentum instead of pressure to achieve agreement.

iv. Give them the time to decide - Remember to give them time to understand that the proposed agreement is beneficial to them.

"Walk slowly if you want to arrive at a job well done sooner."

Augustus, Roman Emperor

The challenge is to persuade them to cross the obstacles and resistances, without putting pressure. It is creating a golden bridge to move forward. To build a golden bridge, ideally, a mediator should be used. In your absence, the challenge is to mediate your agreements to guide the opponent towards your goals.

To build the golden bridge:

1. **Involve the other party** - The bridge makes the other party's YES easier because it involves it. Negotiation is not just a technical exercise to solve problems, but a dynamic process in which everyone has to participate and form agreements jointly.

To involve the other party, ask her ideas and points of view and work around them. You must choose the points that seem most constructive and hence direct the negotiation. You can also launch an idea and ask the other party to comment on it, for example: *"How would you improve it?" Is there any way to make it more beneficial for you, without harming me? They can be offered an alternative: "At 10:00 a.m. Is it a good time to see us? "*

Tell me, and I may hear

Teach me, and I might remember

Involve me in the process, and I will definitely do it!

Benjamin Franklin

Some limiting presumptions that make it difficult for us to see the interests of the other party, and be able to reach them:

    a. **Everything the other party wants is money or something equally tangible** - we overlook intangible needs such as belonging, autonomy, recognition, etc.

    b. **We assume that their needs are opposite to ours**.

    c. **We believe that we can not meet your needs, without thwarting our** – It assumes a mentality of shortage or "fixed foot" - Granting something to the other party, means that it touches me less. You can expand the cake for example: by making a low-cost agreement for us and high profits for them. Also, use a "yes / then" formula. For example: "What do you say if I make my initial fee of $ 10,000 as a base, but if your sales increase 20% in the next six months, then do you add $ 10,000 bonus?".

    d. **That the other part is irrational** – *"my boss is crazy, I cannot deal with him "* Put yourself in the shoes of the other party. Identify your objections and meet your needs, while also meeting our needs.

As a negotiator, it is your job to help the counterpart to be granted without making him feel challenged. *(Back away without backing down).*

Some techniques to achieve this last include:

a. **"The other person was originally fine, but circumstances have now changed."**

b. **Call a mediator, an independent expert** – Something that is initially unacceptable to us at a given time may be acceptable if it comes from a mediator - Such mediator may come up with a proposal that is difficult to reject by the other party.

c. **Use standards that are fair in the absence of a mediator.**

d. **Help write the victory speech of the other party** – write on a page what you think the other party can say when describing and justifying the proposed agreement. Ask yourself what you can offer, what might sound like "victory" without compromising your interests, ask yourself how you can project the agreement in a positive way. Anticipate what will be the criticisms of the other party to arm it with persuasive arguments. The problem can be addressed as an opportunity for the other party if we emphasize the potential benefits for that part. It is better when the other party identifies himself with an opportunity than with a problem. Even if the solution is our idea, let the other party take part of the credit.

EFFECTIVE NEGOTIATING STRATEGIES - NEGOTIATING TACTICS AND DEFENSES

Strategy 1: Flinching (The moan)

The strategy: it consists of shuddering when someone says their terms and conditions, (for example the price). The immediate moan is aimed at removing the opponent's address and lowering their expectations regarding the possibility that we accept their terms.

The tactic: it is precisely that: to shudder and complain as the terms indicate. It is often accompanied by expressions such as: "You must be kidding"…

The best defense is: to justify the reason for the terms and conditions established. Another defense is silence. Silence until the other person desists in opposing and accepting. Like that famous children's game: The first one to speak, loses.

Strategy 2: The Budget

The strategy: It consists of letting the opponent know that you want to buy the product or service that is offered, but that the budget does not allow it. This strategy is ideal when we are hiring someone's services. It also allows us to achieve the sympathy of the contractor, which we will use later in our favor.

The tactic: is to say something kind or gentle about the product or service first, that way the other person does not have to be defensive. Then you let him know that you want to buy the good or service, but that the budget only allows us to spend up to a certain amount of money.

The best defense is to understand that most budgets are NOT written in stone. As a seller, you can establish a payment plan or some combination of consideration that justifies the transaction.

Strategy 3: The selection of cherries

The strategy It is handy when you have to buy a variety of things at once. The goal is to obtain an initial discount price for the entire package and then buy only the cheapest items in each supplier's kit.

The tactic is to compare the offers of each supplier of the set of things that you want to buy, asking for a discount for the complete package. After examining, those things that are most economical are chosen from each supplier.

The best defense is: never give the individual price of each thing when you are giving a discount price on the complete package. Stay firm in saying that the only way to honor those prices is to buy the whole set.

Strategy 4: The pressure of the date (The offer expires)

The strategy: We are used to meeting dates every day. In this case, the whole idea is to force the opponent to decide within a specific time.

The tactic is to say something like: "We are planning to decide within the next x days, if we do not have an answer from you for tomorrow (for example), we will have to contact your competitor." In the world of the Internet we see it every day: "Buy now at this discount price because tomorrow the discount will no longer be available."

The best defense is: understand some deadlines are real, others are false. Do not give up quickly before the imposition of deadlines. Ask for as much time as you need to be able to make the decision. In the case of a seller, if you are establishing a deadline to fulfill an offer, ask him why that date and not another. If the answer does not make sense, surely it is false. If your opponent shows that the deadline is real, you face the dilemma of making a decision on the best possible business under the circumstances or getting out of the transaction.

Strategy 5: Ascent and descent

The strategy consists of having the opponent negotiate with people of different hierarchies, forcing the opponent to negotiate, again and again, thus weakening his position and strengthening the person who uses the strategy.

The tactic is frequently used by large corporations, where it assigns several people to deal with the problem, where the first person has limited authority to negotiate, the second person will have a little more power to negotiate, and so on. When it comes time to talk about dollars, they send back the lowest order to negotiate. They use phrases such as: "I am not authorized to offer more than what I have already offered."

The best defense is: asking beforehand if the person has the necessary and sufficient authority to make decisions. Let your opponents know you will not accept last minute tricks. That is, attack the problem before it occurs. If after the negotiations have begun, the other party tries to implement this strategy, declare that it is a trick on the part of its opponent and that it will not allow it.

Strategy 6: Upss ....! We already did it or "It's better to ask for forgiveness than to ask for permission."

The strategy It is used by many lawyers to sue first and then negotiate. It puts them in a favorable position, where the other person has little to do about it.

The tactic is to perform the work before defining the final conditions of the negotiation. For example, a mechanic who repairs a car before telling the owner how much the repair would cost.

The best defense is to: establish control from the beginning. Ask for detailed estimates from the beginning, before any work is done. Let the other party know that they must not take any action before reaching an agreement (preferably in writing).

Strategy 7: Deadlock

The strategy consists of taking advantage of the fact that many people consider it a failure to find a dead end in the negotiation process. They feel that it is a lack of skills to negotiate effectively. However, there is nothing wrong in arriving at some point at a deadlock in the negotiation process. We must keep that in mind. In general, whoever uses this strategy wants the other party to create such a thing, in such a way that it admits "its failure" and is willing to make concessions.s.

The tactic is to say something like: It seems that we are coming to a standstill. The most skilled will not accuse you of being responsible for such a situation. Usually, the other party will wait for you to say what plans you have to get out of that situation.

The best defense is to say something like this: "Since we have both worked so hard to find solutions, I would hate to see our withdrawal from this negotiation empty-handed. Why do not we agree to leave established those points in which we have already reached an initial agreement, and we meet again next week to discuss the missing aspects we need to reach an agreement?

Using this defense, I have seen controversies reduced from hundreds of thousands of dollars to just a couple of hundred dollars, to be finally resolved in the next round of talks.

Strategy 8: Good Cop, Bad Cop

The strategy consists of weakening the opponent's strength by exposing two different types of opponents: an aggressive and critical person and another understanding person. This strategy, together with the technique of the superior authority, was used by my parents every day with me every time I asked permission to go out and play somewhere.

The tactic: It's commonly seen in the movies, where the bad police interrogate and threaten the suspect, once he has told him everything bad that can happen to him, he leaves the interrogation room, the good cop staying with the person. This good policeman ingratiates himself with him and explains that the only way he has to help him is by collaborating with what the bad police demands.

This strategy is also classic in sales, where the seller would say something like: "For me, I would close the business right now, but my boss does not allow me to do it for less than x figure."

Another classic example occurs when a couple is buying, where one of the parties is interested in the product, while the other is disinterested and willing to leave. The seller, to avoid losing business, ends up accepting special concessions, to ingratiate himself with the apathetic person.

The best defense If you are negotiating with a single person, you must negotiate directly with the one with the highest authority (with the bad police). Another extraordinarily effective way is to assume that both people are in the same position: "Since you speak on behalf of both, I assume that your partner agrees with everything you say." Another completely different defense is to recognize the differences and to claim: "Since it seems that you two do not want the same thing, the best thing is that we meet at another time, once the two of you have managed to reach an agreement." Believe me; this last defense is extremely effective!

Strategy 9: The Pressure of Expectation ("You have to do better")

The strategy: It consists of making you believe that the offer you submitted is not good enough.

The tactic is precisely to say to him: "You are going to have to do it better than that." In this way, not only has he let you know that he is not satisfied with the offer presented but at the same time, he has protected his negotiation strategy by not disclosing a specific amount and forcing the other person to make a counteroffer.

The best defense is reasoning and justifying the business as something more than just the price. Other factors such as service, honesty, reliability, and quality are also relevant conditions in the transaction. N those cases where we are the buyers and the other party tries to apply the strategy to us, we can simply reply with the question "Why?" That way we put the ball on the competitor's court.

Strategy 10: This is my final offer

The strategy It consists of letting you know not only that it is your final offer, but that you are willing to close the business. The idea is for the other person to accept the offer, for the hope of the tacit commitment to close the business. The strategy must be used once it takes time in the negotiation process and not at the beginning, because in that way it will have a more significant emotional impact.

The tactic is to let know that this would be if final offer. Usually, each time a negotiator uses it, he leaves the door open to continue the negotiation.

The best defense is: As we have already said, in general, the person usually leaves an open door to continue with the negotiation process. Look for signs that tell you that this door exists and that it is open. Words like: "Probably, unless, if anything," are signs of such an opportunity. The best solution in these cases is to propose new options, as many as possible.

Strategy 11: Higher Authority

The strategy It is commonly used in sales. Typically the seller will let you know that before accepting the proposed offer, you will need the approval of the manager. It is also very used by our parents: "Ask your mom (dad)." This strategy can sometimes be easily confused with The strategy of the good cop, the bad cop and with The strategy of ascent and descent.

The tactic It is incredibly useful at the end of the negotiation process, where all the terms have already been exposed and have been tentatively accepted. The seller might say something like, "Well, these terms look pretty good to me, but now I have to present them to my boss and get his approval." Different types of Higher Authority can be used, such as husband or wife, a friend, parents, the boss, the board of directors, among others. Sometimes they really intervene in the negotiation, in other cases, it is just an excuse to buy time and be able to return with a counteroffer.

The best defense is: asking in advance and from the beginning to negotiate with the person who makes the final decision, the one with the highest authority. Let him know that you need a response from the highest authority for a specific date.

Another defense is to suggest that you have the opportunity to negotiate a better deal with one of your competitors, you could say something like: "I do not want to lose the offer your competitor has made to me, so I need an answer from you right now."

Strategy 12: Low ball

The strategy it consists in presenting, from the outset, the lowest possible bid, to lower the expectations of the opponent (in the case that the buyer is the one who makes it.) Alternatively, on the contrary, present the lowest and tentative offer possible for the person to fall and want to do business with us, and then discover that this offer is subject to terms that are sometimes unreasonable. The mortgage bank does it very often when they advertise in the newspapers.

The tactic consists of offering the lowest possible price, with the promise that more business will be done or that it will be possible to close it quickly.

The best defense would depend upon whether you are the seller or the buyer.

<u>When you are the seller</u>, do not bother with such a low offer. Let the buyer know what the benefits of your product or service, which justifies the price requested is.

<u>When you are the buyer,</u> and the seller appears with this super mega irresistible low bid, be very careful. Usually, if it sounds too good to be true, it's because it's too good to be true. Ask about the details of the offer. Find what the conditions that must be given so that the same offer is fulfilled are.

In personal negotiations, make a strict comparison between your opponent's offer and what you consider fair. Let the other party know that you are looking for a fair and reasonable agreement.

Strategy 13: Freebies (The Salami).

The strategy: Because people tend to be impatient negotiators, they often give concessions on minor issues, only to get the deal crystallized as soon as possible. The conscious opponent of this will try to get you to make concessions from the beginning in those little things. In other words, you will eat the whole salami, bite by bite, without you noticing, one slice at a time.

The tactic is very effective once an initial agreement has been reached. Once an agreement has been achieved in the primary business, it is requested to add the most to the original transaction. Some people are excellent at this strategy. For example, once they buy something, say a computer, they request that something like some software is added, or a larger monitor or a free printer, in short, something. Sometimes the seller accepts, without realizing that this concession sometimes equals as much as the primary business.

The best defense is: Refusing to give the nail, as quickly as the one who asks for it. If you remain firm enough in your refusal, the one requesting the freebie will desist. Another excellent alternative is to have a price list (in writing) available. It gives legitimacy and people are more reluctant to challenge a price if they see that it is written.

Strategy 14: The Auction

The strategy consists of putting the others to compete among themselves, in such a way that you make sure that you will achieve the best offer.

The tactic It is usually the citing the competitors at the same time. Let them know that you are requesting a quote from others and that it is not a delusion or bluff. They will be forced to present their best offer if they want to take the business.

The best defense it is: to indicate the reason for the terms and the conditions of its product is superior to the one of its competition. Separate yourself from your competition by pointing out what makes your service or product superior. Give added value instead of making concessions in the price.

Strategy 15: Take it or leave it

The strategy It works when one does not have any incentive to continue with the transaction if another concession is granted. It is also useful when you want to avoid creating a precedent that may harm future relationships, so it is preferable that the business falls before accepting more concessions. It also serves when you want to test the strength of the opponent, and we have reached a point that we feel we have exhausted the options. In general, it is accompanied by a deadline to make good the offer.

The tactic is: the experienced negotiator will not use the words "Take it or leave it," on the contrary, he will find a way to get the message through without it sounding like a threat. In general, they will back their position with legitimate reasons. He will use phrases like: "Unfortunately that's the most I can offer," "I'm afraid I'll be forced to report it if he refuses to comply with company policies." This strategy is prevalent in criminal cases and also in cases involving real estate transactions, including divorce cases.

The best defense is: ignore the fact that we are considering a "Take it or leave it." Keep raising alternatives (if we have them). Another is to say something like: "I cannot accept this offer in the way it is currently planned," or If you are not willing to look for a better alternative, I was forced to look for someone else."

Strategy 16: What if ...?

The strategy behind this question is to seek as much information as possible from our opponent. The answers we give to these types of questions reveal more about ourselves than we would like to show.

The tactic is to ask: "What would happen if we change this or that condition, how would it affect the price or the final result?

The best defense is to answer this type of question with another question. An example of such rebuttal would be: Why do you ask? Do you get a special discount buying that part for yourself? Remember: Answer with another question that gives you more information.

Strategy 17: The phony problem solver

The strategy: the "win-win" philosophy leaves the door open for pseudo-win-win deals. Many people act as if they want to help you, but in reality, they just want you to put all your cards on the table and disarm.

The tactic used by the experts is to use expressions like: "Let me see how I can help you," "Let's put the cards on the table to see how we can make this work for both."

The best defense is to: recognize this type of people because although they express that they want to put the cards on the table, they do not reveal anything or very little about themselves. Limit the amount of information you give. Ask questions to know about the other person. Understand that you are facing a challenge and do not neglect yourself.

Strategy 18: The Lure

The strategy consists in seeking to distract your attention and prevent you from realizing what are the real challenges of negotiation by making you believe that the person is interested in something that in reality has little interest for her.

The tactic: The person makes a low offer but includes an additional condition (the lure). The other person loses so much time in eliminating that further concession that distracts his attention from the real significant problem: the supply goes down. For example: Make a low bid and include household items. The person will lose so much energy and time in the equipment that they may be distracted from the actual relevant point: the low bid.

The best defense is: knowing what you exactly want from the deal and not making any concession in those points that are neuralgic for you in the negotiation. Those points that would make it preferable to withdraw from the negotiation if you give them.

Strategy 19: Friendship or family relationships

The strategy: Negotiations with a friend or family member are usually charged with an emotional element because the person will appeal to the relationship to demand extraordinary or unique concessions.

The tactic: The opponent will use this strategy by saying something like: "Look, you and I have been friends for a long time," or "If you really care about me ..." The person will use this strategy when he considers the point more important than the relationship or when he considers the relationship important enough and strong enough to withstand the onslaught of emotional extortion.

The best defense en: Avoid doing business with family and friends at all costs. If this is not possible, and you are forced to carry out a negotiation with a relative or friend, look for alternatives that allow you to keep the relationship, while at the same time satisfying both parties. Do not allow yourself to be offended or manipulated by this strategy. Ask yourself if friendship is really at risk. Keep your emotions under control at all times.

Strategy 20: Discouragement and Indifference

The strategy: The essayist Juan Montalvo once said: "There is nothing harder than the softness of indifference" How right are his words!

The tactic: There is a story of the Rockefeller family that tells that one day an investor came to talk with John Rockefeller, Jr. The investor started the conversation by saying:

- "Well, how much do you want for your property?" Rockefeller replied:

- "Mr. Morgan, I think there must be an error. I'm not here to sell anything; I think it's you who wants to buy something "...

In expressing his indifference, Rockefeller limited the bargaining power of his adversary.

The best defense is: find what motivates your opponent, instead of the points to negotiate itself. Say something like: "I see it reluctant to want to do business, could you ask why?" "Maybe it is not the right time for either of you to want to carry out this negotiation." You must then look for new alternatives that overcome the barriers of negotiation initially imposed by this strategy.

Strategy 21: The commitment

The strategy: When the person does not have better alternatives, he resorts to commitment. It's an easy way to avoid negotiating. It implies that both parties have to accept sacrifices.

The tactic: People often say: "split the difference in half." Any alternative that does not allow you to achieve the highest amount of what you want is a commitment.

The best defense is: Introduce new alternatives You can comment: "If we split the difference we both lose, what do you think is better this alternative ...". Another good defense is to use The strategy of the "low ball" to lower your expectations of reaching a commitment to divide the losses in half.

Strategy 22: The Stonewall

The strategy: This strategy is very similar to the strategy of indifference. It is distinguished in that the person adopts a rigid and inflexible attitude, at the same time that raises an open refusal to negotiate, beyond that point. Nor should be confused with The strategy number seven (Deadlock), because it has not reached a deadlock in the negotiation, but that the person is raising an aspiration, which is not willing to give so easily.

The tactic: People are often planted in a seemingly firm and inflexible position. For example some requirement, deadline, among others. The person will say something like: "That is the final price."

The best defense is: Test your seriousness by ignoring The tactic, changing the subject or continue talking about the problem as if you had not heard The tactic. In the process introduce new alternatives.

Another excellent defense: is to interpret a stonewall, as if it were an aspiration and direct attention towards the solution of the problem. We can say something like: "we all have aspirations, the management is under great pressure for the ups and downs of the economy, and I know that you would like to cut wages but if we look at the merits, realistically, what other company is paying its employees for the same job?"

Also, if there is a Deadline, use it as a target, say: "to meet your deadline, we will need your help."

Ask many questions. If they tell you that the price is final, then ask: "Can I have financing?" If they answer yes, it means that they are flexible.

Strategy 23: Attacks

The strategy: This strategy is hazardous. Given the lack of capacity to negotiate the substantive aspects of the problem, the person will change the focus of attention, from the solution of the problem of attacking the person with whom it is negotiating.

The tactic: People will frequently show an adverse animosity towards the other party, expressing themselves in personalist terms. They will stop debating ideas and begin to use epithets, or on the contrary, they will irrationally claim that what is being proposed "is a lack of respect."

The best defense is to ignore them, pretend that we did not listen. If the other party sees that the attack is being ignored, they will probably give up. If it does not work to ignore it, it must be reinterpreted as a friendly attack.

We must put on patience, like a knight's armor coated with Teflon®. The important thing is to redirect the focus towards the solution of the problem. Direct the issue in controversy from the past to the future, from what is wrong to what can be done to solve the problem. Change from "you and me" to a "we." Instead of sitting face to face, sit next to him. As we have said before, it is difficult to argue with someone who is on your side.

Strategy 24: Tricks

The strategy: This strategy is one of the most difficult to counterattack. The person will appear at the negotiating table with a hidden agenda and will not show their true intentions until it is too late to react.

The tactic: The person, at the end of the process, will "take out of the hat" aspects that were not initially on the negotiating table.

The best defense is: Try to reveal the trick, following the current. We should ask questions to prove sincerity. Respond as if the other party was negotiating in good faith. The key is to ask clarifying questions. If a contradiction is detected, do not announce it immediately, just act confused, ask for more explanations. You can ask questions for which we already have the answers. This strategy is the favorite of lawyers during depositions in litigious processes.

We must put them in the dilemma of cooperating in designing and administering a test that allows us to corroborate whether the other party would agree to accept a reasonable requirement to be genuinely collaborating. If we detect the trick, we use it to our advantage.

Remember the saying: Play dumb like a fox.

From the outset, we must investigate who has the authority to make decisions, to avoid listening: "That does not depend on me ...."

If all the above does not work, we must renegotiate the rules of the game, (which are supposed to have been clearly established at the beginning of the negotiation process).

It is important to note at this point that in any negotiation process two negotiations are actually carried out:

a. **Of substance of content** – terms, and conditions in dollars and cents

b. **Rules of the game** – how it will take place - usually they stay tacit, but they must be explicit.

   i. To negotiate on the negotiation rules, you must identify interests, generate options on how to negotiate better, establish fair negotiation standards. "We have to recognize that together we can meet the needs of both..."

Finally remember to deal with the tactics without appearing, personally attacking the other party.

The turning point: is when you change the trading game by position to a negotiation of problem-solving. The key is to take what the other party says and direct it against the problem and not against yourself. Seeing the opponent as an associate in the positions, and that these positions he adopts, offer us an opportunity to talk about the problem.

Make sure the other part is removed from the table with a good flavor. Moreover, finally, remember:

Don't get mad,

Don't get even,

Get what you want!

THE GOOD HUMOR AS THE UNIVERSAL DEFENSE

The universal defense against each and every one of the strategies mentioned here is a good sense of humor. Humor makes negotiation easy, without offending anyone.

You don't have to be a comedian, but in a funny way you can tell your opponent that you have recognized the strategy he is using against you: "Ok, I have also used that strategy sometimes in my negotiations."

You must be careful to make that comment without sarcasm and without using an accusatory tone. Let the other know that you are enjoying the negotiation process.

Another powerful defense is the silence. After someone uses a strategy against you, just keep quiet. When you remain silent, your opponent will start to feel uncomfortable and start talking again. That is precisely what you want. The more he tells, the more you will know about him. Also, silence is synonymous with indifference, which will make it him who becomes a "victim" of that negotiation strategy already explained.

An alternative modality to silence is to change the topic of conversation: Keeping quiet about the particular point, but talking about other issues that have nothing to do. Once again, that attitude will reflect that you are indifferent to what is proposed, what that will make the person make new concessions.

The best defense is to know these and other negotiation strategies, not only to use them as negotiation weapons but to prevent them from being used against us. By staying alert and with the mind focused on the desired achievements, you can obtain the expected result.

In general terms, to distract the strategies, it is not necessary to reject them but to transform them into attempts to solve the problem. It is a bit like using judo techniques in the negotiation process, where "non-resistance" constitutes a primordial technical principle.

In the case of the judoka, it "flows" in the strength of its attacker, whether it has been pushed or pulled, since, in this way, the opposite effort is canceled and the expenditure of the energy itself is optimized, at the same time that weakens the attacker's balance.

The most common ways to achieve it are:

1) reinterpret it

2) ignore it

3) prove it

4) expose it

5) negotiate it

In each case, the purpose is the same, to persuade them not to use tactics against us and instead refocus their energies on solving the problem.

B.A.T.N.A .: How to use power as an integral part of negotiation:

BATNA (Best Alternative To a Negotiated Agreement) – It means in simple words, what will be the best alternative, given the possibility that we do not agree to an agreement in the negotiations.

For this, it is imperative to know what the minimum number of conditions we would be willing to accept, that if any of them were not present, it would be preferable to get up from the negotiating table.

That cluster of minimum conditions, commonly known by its term in English as "bottom line" is the barometer that determines when we will apply the BATNA.

An example would be: "If we can not reach an agreement, we will have no choice but to end up in court and the judge decides the amount to pay." It is that option that leads the person to a constructive negotiation and protects your interests in case the negotiation fails.

The BATNA can occur in one of the following modalities:

1. **Unilateral** – By unilaterally withdrawing from the negotiation.

2. **Bilateral** – When we decide in a bi-lateral way that it is preferable to put a stop to the negotiation process. The famous phrase in English: "We agree to disagree." In which case, both parties decide to "live with the consequences of not having reached an agreement," which in most

cases means maintaining the status quo and in other cases, means the intensification of tensions.

3. **Trilateral** - Search for help (Mediation and Arbitration). It is trilateral because it involves a third person in the panorama.

All these options minimize the impact towards the parties. They leave open the possibility of future negotiations.

Do not use the BATNA unless it is strictly necessary. It is better to educate the other party about the consequences of not achieving a mutual agreement, even if it implies giving in and committing.

Here again applies the saying of my father: "Sometimes a bad agreement is better than a good lawsuit." Not only because of the economic cost of litigation but it is up to the parties to deal with the consequences of the judgment issued by the court, that at times it could turn out to be much more unfavorable than the worst scenario that could have been achieved through a negotiation process.

To determine what is the best alternative to a negotiated agreement, we must ask ourselves questions designed to analyze the impact of not reaching an agreement.

Remember, a warning may be more effective than using the BATNA, but without sounding a threat. And you may wonder, what is the difference between a warning and a threat?:

The warning is an objective and respectful announcement of the dangers that lie ahead. In the warning, the information is presented neutrally and objectively.

The threat is a <u>subjective announcement</u> of your intentions to cause pain or punishment to the opponent, and that seeks confrontation.

It is suggested that to force a decision; the warning should be presented accompanied by a deadline for decision making. (For example the meeting of the Board).

If the other party ignores the warning, then you have to prove your BATNA, credibly. For example, if our BATNA is going to court, we can show you by bringing a lawyer to the negotiations or by writing a letter written by your legal representative.

As we have already said, one way to demonstrate the BATNA is to withdraw from the negotiation. Say: *"I do not agree with the way we are negotiating, here is my phone number, let me know when you are willing to negotiate."*

The idea is to allow the other party an escape route and that the escape route is to negotiate.

If none of the above works, you have to use the BATNA. However, preferably to the smallest extent possible, to avoid unnecessary reactions from the other party.

The most effective way to neutralize is to involve other people, identifying potential allies. A potential ally may be a close associate of the other party. By the bond that unites them, the opponent listens more to his own.

These third parties help promote negotiation. Sometimes, just knowing that there is someone else watching is enough to take a person to the negotiating table. These can help mediate, seeking to help understand common interests.

Unless, of course, we have already exhausted all the alternatives and we have no choice but to "burn the boats" and defend ourselves with all the legal tools at our disposal.

An imposed result will be an unstable one. The most stable results are usually achieved through negotiation.

Once you succeed in taking the other party to the desired terms, you have to translate those good intentions into a firm and lasting agreement. Design a deal that will lead the other party to keep his word and protect you if he does not.

If the other party is offended and says: "Trust me, answer, I trust you, but it is a normal procedure." If the other party breaks the agreement, a dispute resolution procedure must be established in advance.

PSYCHOLOGICAL FACTORS AND HOW TO FACE THEM

The psychological factor is an essential and critical aspect of the effective negotiation process. Its importance is evident when we answer the following question: **If effective negotiation offers so many advantages, how is it possible that it is so underutilized?** Those who best negotiate, understand their own mental attitudes and those of their counterparts very well.

The ideas presented below will help overcome the possible psychological barriers that may arise in the effective negotiation process while helping them to obtain better results.

• **Be aware of psychological factors.** The field of the mind is subtle and therefore sometimes underestimated. The awareness of the psychological considerations that comprise effective negotiation can be of great help for possible barriers that may arise.

Concrete steps must be taken to achieve the parties actively cooperate between them. One of the most important steps is to realize that there is a better way to interact than the traditional negotiating approach where only one party wins, and the other party necessarily loses. If the pressure to win can be removed in a blind competitive manner, the parties are encouraged to cooperate.

For this, we must always keep in mind specific basic rules that are very useful not only for effective delegation but all types of interpersonal relationships. We have adopted these principles in this book from Neuro-linguistic Programming and listed them below:

1. Respect the world's model of others.

2. The meaning of the communication is the response obtained.

3. The mind and body affect each other.

4. The words we use do not represent the event or the object. The map is not the territory, nor the dinner menu.

5. The most critical information of a person is their behavior.

6. The behavior presented is the best alternative of a person, if he had other alternatives whose behaviors were more appropriate, this (the behavior) would change.

7. The person is NOT their behavior. Do not label people.

8. There are no inept people, only incapacitating states. Everyone has the resources for success.

9. I am in charge of my mind. Therefore I am responsible for my results (achievements).

10. The person with the greatest flexibility of behavior (variety of requirements) controls is the system.

11. There is no such thing as failure, there are only results.

12. There are no tough customers, just inflexible communicators.

13. All procedures must increase resources (alternatives).

NEGOTIATION

As we see, the presuppositions in Neuro-linguistic Programming (NLP) are extremely useful when negotiating, looking for results that are ecological, that is: win-win.

WHO HAS THE GREATEST EGO? THE POWER PARADOX

"The harder it is for your opponents to say no,

The harder it will be for them to say yes. "

In the search to lead the adversary to accept our terms, we run the risk of falling into the delicate and perilous game of threatening the opponent to fall back. In these cases, our counterparts usually decide to resist and fight.

The big dilemma is how to use the power to lead the opponent to accept our terms without ending up in a fight? The most common mistake is to abandon the game of looking for a common solution to the problem and entering into the game of power in which the dialogue turns into threats.

In this stage of struggle for power, we stop seeing the position of the other party, by insisting on their own and we seek to force them to act. This is a grave mistake because in the process of the fight, relations with the other side are destroyed and all possibility of dialogue and constructive negotiation process. And as the old adage says: "One eye for an eye, and we all go blind."

So how can we overcome the game of who has the biggest ego? Simple! We must make it easy for them to say yes, while at the same time we must make it difficult for them to say no.

1. Make it easy to say yes - it requires using problem-solving negotiation.

2. Make it difficult to say no - it requires using power delicately and intelligently. Including the power of persuasion.

There is no need to choose between the two alternatives, both can and should be used: Power can be used as an integral part of the negotiation of problem-solving, to seek mutual satisfaction, to come to reason.

We must use the power wisely to educate the opponent and invite him to act as if he miscalculated how to reach his goals, without imposing our terms and that way we can reach a mutual agreement.

EPILOGUE

Virtually all aspects of life are affected by the need to negotiate. Daily examples and their consequences may go unnoticed. The house where you live, the car you drive, the work you have, what you receive from wages, what you pay for rent, what you pay for your car, the clothes you wear, what you paid for those clothes. Virtually everything in this life is affected by our ability to negotiate effectively.

No matter what excuse we give, the most significant barrier to highly effective negotiation is ourselves. It is in our hands to develop the necessary skills to achieve excellence when negotiating effectively.

That is why we have wanted to offer you in this book a comprehensive manual that will help you develop these skills. We hope we have reached our goal.

If you want more information about how you can participate in our seminars, training, VIP group and our exclusive personalized consulting service, you can visit our website.

Remember that there are only two types of people, those who take the lead to seek improvement and those who choose to remain immobile while the change moves them further and further away from the triumph. In which group do you want to be?

BIBLIOGRAPHY

- Alec Mackenzie. <u>Gerencia en Acción</u>
  Codado, Caracas, 1972.
- Francisco Diez. <u>El Arte de Negociar</u>
  Instituto Nacional Demócrata.
- Leon C. Megginson & others. <u>Management, Concepts & Applications</u>
- Harper & Row Publishers, New York, 1983.
- Michael E. Gerber. <u>The E Myth Revisited</u>
  Harper Business, New York, 1995.
- Bernardo Magnini. <u>Using NLP Techniques for Meaning Negotiation</u>
  Centro para la Riqueza Científica y Tecnológica, Italia, 2002.
- Gerard Nierenberg. <u>The Art of Negotiating</u>
  Negotiation Institute, New York, 2007.
- Robert Diltz. <u>The Fourth Position</u>
- Mare Koit. <u>Dialogue Management in Agreement negotiation Process</u>
  Tartu University, Estonia, 2001.
- Susan Wherspann. <u>Negotiation- The Basics</u>
- Francisco J. Sánchez y otros. <u>Preparándose para Negociar</u>
  CMI International Group, 1999
- William Ury. <u>Sin Comunicación no hay Negociación</u>
- Microsoft® Encarta® 2006. © 1993-2005 Microsoft Corporation.

OTHER BOOKS BY IVAN REMUS, PE, ESQ.

The lawyer Ivan Remus has several books to his repertoire within the theme of Management and Leadership, among which are:

Negotiation.

Delegation.

Letters from a Divorced Father - The Other Side of the Moon.

Likewise, a series of books on the vital topic of Self-Help and Motivation is currently being developed.

The complete list can be found at www.ivanremus.com

It is also important to note that all your books are available in both English and Spanish languages.

ABOUT THE AUTHOR

Ivan Remus is a renowned lawyer and engineer who holds the Master Practitioner designation in Neuro-linguistic Programming (NLP) and has admitted to practice law in at least ten federal courts, including the Supreme Court of the United States (SCOTUS).

His successful career in the legal, engineering, real estate, and academic fields is extensive and focuses on business consulting. Mr. Remus, who has personally pledged to contribute to the practice of law through his private practice and academic legacy, has enjoyed a reputation as a passionate and dedicated executive, with extensive experience and proven success in complicated negotiation processes.

He is also the author of numerous books in the fields of business administration and leadership, as well as in the area of self-help. You can follow him on his blog: www.IvanRemus.com

THANK YOU!

Ivan Thank you for buying and reading this book. I hope you find it an interesting and useful guide on how to achieve success when negotiating every aspect of your professional and personal life.

Before leaving, would it be okay with you if I ask you a small favor? Could you take a moment and leave a brief comment of one or two lines on the website where you bought this book? Your review can help others decide what to read next. I would be greatly appreciated by many other readers.

RESOURCES

If you want additional information, on how you can participate in our seminars, training, VIP group and our exclusive personalized consulting service, you can visit our website. Let me know if you are interested in me coming to your city to give a talk or training on this or any other topic.

www.ivanremus.com

www.ingramcontent.com/pod-product-compliance
Lightning Source LLC
Chambersburg PA
CBHW030454220526
45464CB00006B/2536